Investing In Stock Market For Beginners

Understanding the basics of how to make money with stocks

Neil Hoechlin

http://bit.ly/neilhoechlin

No part of this book may be reproduced or transmitted in any form whatsoever, electronic, or mechanical, including photocopying, recording, or by any informational storage or retrieval system without express permission from the author

Copyright © 2016 JNR Publishing Group

All rights reserved

ISBN-13: 978-1541294318
ISBN-10: 1541294319

INTRODUCTION

What are Stocks?

Basic Terms

The Stock Market

Market Capitalization

Financial Statements

Here are seven popular financial ratios:

Stock Market Timeline

Investing in the Stock market

Stock Market Indices

WHAT YOU NEED TO DO BEFORE YOU INVEST

Picking the Right Stock

Types of Stocks

Before you invest I advise you do the following:

Stocks Investment Strategies

Financial Advisors

Getting Started

WHILE YOU ARE INVESTING

Day Trading

Short Term Trading

Medium Trading

Long Term Trading

MAKING THE RIGHT INVESTMENT

When to Buy:

When to Sell:

BAD INVESTMENT BEHAVIORS

CONCLUSION

INTRODUCTION

Every form of trading most always follows a similar pattern. A trader buys low, sells high, keeps the profit, keeps customers satisfied, and keeps a record. Trading in stocks is also a just the run of the mill form of trading in this regard. The only difference is that you don't have to do the trading yourself. Sometimes, people do it for you with your money but you must always have knowledge of what to buy and sell, and at what price you want to sell them.

Usually when you trade in goods, you go through a process of acquisition. This includes the logistics of transporting your goods to where you want them, storing them, and sometimes, transporting them to your buyers; all of which you have to be involved in. Trading in stocks does away with all these operational details as stocks are not tangible objects. You simply acquire your stocks, and you have a figure with your name beside it as evidence that you own them. You don't need to transport them and you don't need to store them in the warehouse. These days, you don't even need to leave your house or contact the buyer before you sell. You simply look at the value of stocks you want to sell and sell them with the click of a mouse.

Stocks, also known as company shares, are one of the most popular kinds of investments. They are higher in risks than other forms of investment like bonds but are also usually higher in returns. Therefore, it is advisable to have a considerable part of your investment in stocks. If a company is doing well, you want to take part in their success. Stock prices tend to fluctuate based on supply and demand. You can make money by an increase in a stock's share price or if a company pays a dividend.

This eBook shows you the fundamentals of investing and trading in stocks. Whether you are trying to increase and accumulate your money for future use, or you are looking at making some money in the short term, this eBook will be of help. It has been written in a very simple way to describe what the stock market is all about, what to know before you invest, and how to invest.

What are Stocks?

A stock is a partial ownership investment. Also called shares, stocks are the parts in which the ownership of a business entity has been broken down into. These parts are then sold to people who can buy them and therefore, become stakeholders to the business entity. They contribute in a limited way to decision making based on the size of their shares and also share in the profits of the company in form of dividends.

Think about a business entity as a cake sliced up into numerous pieces and each piece sold to individuals. Each piece is a part of the main cake and also a cake on its own. Each piece of cake is a share in this regard. Investment in stocks is called an equity investment.

Basic Terms

Before we go into details about stocks and the stock market, we need to get familiar with some commonly used words in investment.

Asset

An asset is an item in which the investor puts his money to enjoy the benefits of said resource. Typically the investor hopes that its value will appreciate and it will bring returns directly or indirectly. Assets can be tangible or intangible. Stocks are intangible assets.

Investment Portfolio

This is the total sum of all your investments, both in nature and in value. Investors can diversify their portfolio by investing in a variety of assets. For instance, you can have 30% of your investment in bonds, 30% in stocks, and the remaining 40% in real estate.

Holdings

Your holdings are the specific assets in your investment portfolio.

Asset class

An asset class is a group of similar assets, e.g. stocks and bonds. Assets in the same class usually have different risks and different returns for the investor even though they are similar in nature. For instance, if you invest in an IPO or initial stocks offering by Facebook, while buying a couple of stocks from Apple, what you are doing is investing in different assets of the same class (safe stocks of highly established companies). While the two assets are stocks, they would differ in value, risks and return on investment.

Equity

This refers to investment in an asset in form of partial ownership of an entity. Stocks are the most common form of equity investment.

Securities

A security is a tradable financial asset. It represents the asset that you have invested in, especially if it is in bonds or stocks. Bonds are called debt securities while stocks are called equity securities. Bonds are IOUs or debts. You are in effect becoming the lender to the issuer of a bond (corporation, government etc).

Return on Investment (ROI)

This is the value you get back for investing your money in an asset. Your returns can be in form of increased value when you sell your asset in the future or in form of regular profits or dividends.

The Stock Market

Basically, the stock market is a system where shares, derivatives, options and similar financial instruments from different companies are issued, bought, and then sold.

All across the world, there are stock markets where millions of stocks from hundreds of companies are traded on a daily basis. There is a lot of speculation in the stock market. There are investors who buy shares of a company, in the hopes that it will perform well in the future. There are also investors who sell shares of a company, when they believe that the company will perform poorly in the future or if this is the best time to cash out on the gains.

In the US, we have the New York Stock Exchange (NYSE) where public stocks from American companies are traded. The trade in stocks and other securities is regulated by the government through the Securities Exchange Commission (SEC). In the past, stocks have been a highly attractive investment in the US because the share price of most traded companies kept increasing. The market was bullish in the 1990s through the early 21st century.

This trend started reversing with the bear market of 2000 to 2002 as the tech bubble burst but markets hit a new high in 2007 with soaring stock prices. Stocks crashed abruptly in 2008, not only in the United States but across the world. Today, stocks continue to be a widely popular and smart investment choice. The market is beginning to look good again. Both the S&P 500 and NASDAQ are showing good indices. Analysts hope the positive trend will last.

Due to the frequent bombardment of information by the media, the market is more volatile than it used to be. However, if you want to be a successful investor, do not follow the headlines, but the trend lines and fundamentals. The perceived value of a company can be artificially manipulated and bloated by several percent! However, its true value may actually be just $2 per share, even though the market is trading it for $3.50 or higher. If you are new to the game? Stick with companies with justifiable and solid fundamentals instead of volatility in prices easily swayed by public opinion and other market forces. In that way, you are playing safe.

The uncertainty in the stock market makes it risky to invest sometimes, but it is also what makes it highly lucrative to invest in. The changes in price and size of stocks are determined by multiple factors both internal and external. Before you start trading, you must have knowledge of the stock market and understand the forces causing price fluctuations of each company stocks.

Market Capitalization

Market capitalization is one of those terms I used to hear on the late night business news long before I understood the stock market. Even though I had no clue what it was, I always thought it would have to do with size. I wasn't too wrong.

A stock's market capitalization, or market cap for short, is the total dollar value of all the company's outstanding shares. It is calculated by multiplying the current stock price by the number of outstanding shares. In other words, the value of all the shares of the company traded on an exchange. This is how the size of a company is determined. For instance, if a company has 2million shares outstanding, and the value of its shares is $5, its market capitalization is $10million

Companies are separated into three main market caps: large cap, mid cap and small cap. There are other caps such as micro and mega cap, but we will just stick to the main three.

Small cap represents stocks with less than $2 billion dollar capitalization. Mid cap represents stocks with between $2 billion and $10 billion dollar capitalization, and large cap represents stocks with market capitalization over $10 billion. Any company from large cap upwards is called a blue chip. Examples are General Electric and Exxon-Mobil.

Logically, the larger a company's market cap is, the safer its stocks are. Large cap stocks are therefore considered safer than the lower caps because they are more likely to withstand a financial crisis such as an economic or market crash. A good way to think about it is to look at market capitalization as the wooly coat that protects the companies from cold. The thicker the wool, the more likely it is to protect the wearer from the cold of the harsh winter and make him comfortable. Large cap companies are big corporations that have weathered the storm over the years and have remained strong. However, small caps' stocks have a higher potential for growth though generally more unstable. Therefore, if what's most important to you is security, then invest in large caps but if you see a positive trend and want to make some money by buying now and selling in a short term, then you can put your money in the small caps.

Financial Statements

The financial statement is a document that contains the financial records of a company over a period of time. It is important because it shows the status of a company. It reflects profit, growth and assets. Investors study the financial statements of companies to help them make decisions on investments. There are 3 different parts to a company's financial statements.

1. **Balance Sheet**: The balance sheet represents a record of a company's assets, liabilities, and equity at a particular point in time, as in a snapshot. A company's assets are the resources that the business owns or controls at a given point in time. They can include items such as cash, inventory, machinery, buildings, intellectual properties and in some cases, good will.

2. **Income Statement:** It measures a company's performance over a specific time frame. It presents information about revenues, expenses, and profit that was generated as a result of the business' operations for that period.

3. **Statement of Cash Flows**: This represents a record of a business' cash inflows and outflows over a period of time. This includes Operating Cash Flow which is cash generated from day-to-day business operations, cash from investing, as well as the proceeds from the sale of other businesses, equipment, or long-term assets. Also included, is cash from financing -- which measures the flow of cash between a firm and its owners and creditors.

Analysts will typically look at financial ratios to help them make decisions from the financial statement. The ratios are created by calculating the relationship between items on the financial statement with each other and/or outside forces.

Here are seven popular financial ratios:

1. Profit Margin

A metric used to assess a firm's financial health by revealing the proportion of money left over from revenues after accounting for the cost of goods sold. It is basically how much a company makes after subtracting their expenses. The higher the profit margin, the better.

2. EPS Growth Rate

EPS is earning per share. EPS Growth is how much the EPS has grown each year. They compare the current earnings amount with earnings from previous years. Again, the higher the EPS growth rate, the better.

3. Price to Book

It's an estimated ratio used by investors that compares a stock's per-share price to its book value. You can think of book value as the value of a company, if the company was to be liquidated. The lower the price to book, the more undervalued a company is considered.

4. Price to Sales

The Price to Sales ratio measures the price of a company's stock against its annual sales. The lower the price to sales, the more undervalued a company is considered.

5. Price to Earnings (P/E)

Basic earnings per share (EPS) divided into the current stock price. The lower the price to earnings, the more undervalued a company is considered.

6. Return on Equity

Indicates how profitable a company is, by comparing its net income to its average shareholders' equity. It measures how much the shareholders earned for their investment in the company. The higher the ratio percentage, the more efficient management is in utilizing its equity base to generate profits.

7. Debt to Equity

It relates a company's total liabilities to its total shareholders' equity. It is a measurement of how much suppliers, lenders, and creditors have committed to the company versus what the shareholders have committed. A lower debt to equity figure is preferable for a fundamental analyst, as it reflects a company that owes a low amount of debt. This typically means it is more financially sound.

Stock Market Timeline

The stock market operates in 2 typical cycles:

- **Bullish trend**: a period of time characterized by increase in stocks value across the market

- **Bearish trend**: a period of time characterized by a decline in stocks value across the market.

The market crash and subsequent financial crisis of 2008 has been attributed to a bubble bust.

A bubble is a phenomenon whereby market participants drive stock prices above their real value, i.e. their value in relation to a credible system of stock evaluation. When a bubble bursts, there is a sudden reversal in stock value in which stock prices crash to their realistic values. Although the market is looking good now, some analysts are hinting that we might be in a new bubble. Global investor, Marc Faber predicted on CNBC that U.S stocks could fall by 50%.

Investing in the Stock market

Before investing in the stock market, you should know what you want and why you want it. This requires gathering substantial information to help you in deciding.

To succeed in the stock market, you need the following:

- Understanding the reason why you want to invest. Are you buying stocks for appreciation (capital gains) or income (dividends)?
- A good understanding of economics and economic factors that affect stock values.
- A good knowledge of the company you are considering investing in. For instance, is the company profitable? A thorough background company research is in order.
- Choosing the right industry to invest in. Some small companies in a fast moving industry bring good returns.
- Identifying trends and megatrends. Know how to study market indicators for a period of time and identify the patterns and trends.
- Understanding of how events around the world affect the industry, the company and subsequently the stock itself.

- Defining your investment strategy. Higher risk, but higher reward? Or you want to play it safer?

Stock Market Indices

You may have watched business news on TV and seen the reporters quote some technical values associated with names like Dow Jones and NASDAQ, using the values to analyze the state of the stock market. These are stock market indices. A stock market index is a weighted average computed from prices of selected stocks of a segment of the market. It is therefore, a measurement of the value of a section of the market, and is used to describe or form a general picture of that segment and to get an idea of the returns on investments there. I will describe the 3 most popular stock market indices briefly below:

Standard and Poor's 500 (S & P 500)

The S & P 500 stock index is made up of 500 of the most widely traded stocks in the U.S. It represents 805 of the American stock market and is, therefore, a reflection of the entire market. One of the defining characteristics of this index is that it is market capitalization weighed. This means that a relatively small shift in the price of a large company can cause a significant shift in the value of the index. The value of the index also changes relative to the total market value.

Dow Jones Industrial Average (DJIA)

The DJIA reflects the average share price of the stocks of 30 of the largest and most influential companies in the U.S. It is one of the oldest and most widely used and thus globally influential indices in the world. The DJIA was originally determined by adding up the share prices of all 30 companies in the index and dividing it by the number of companies. The method of computing has become more complex in recent times. The DJIA is a price weighed index, which means it is dependent on share price. Because the DJIA reflects the value of about a quarter of the value of the entire market, changes in the index do not significantly affect the entire market but gives a reflection of changes and expectations towards the stocks of big companies.

NASDAQ Composite Index

The NASDAQ stock exchange is the market on which technology stocks are traded. The NASDAQ Composite Index indicates the market capitalization average of all stocks on the NASDAQ stock exchange. In recent times, the Nada market has also included stocks in Financial and insurance industries.

WHAT YOU NEED TO DO BEFORE YOU INVEST

Picking the Right Stock

Knowing what stocks to buy at what time is not rocket science, but you can't be reckless and have to do your research well. It takes a combination of your investment goals, market indices, and economic indicators to invest in the right stocks for you. When an event that reflects instability occurs in a major oil producer like Saudi Arabia for instance, it is expected that oil prices will rise but how that will impact on the stocks of companies in oil and gas is more complex. Those who are great investors know the cause and effect relationships of major events and a master at analysis of the facts on hand. It's beyond the scope of this book, but a combination of experience (simulations and actual money) and the different financial and forecasting techniques and the ability to do technical analysis and of course consulting with the experts such as stock brokers and financial analysts will help you in this regard.

Types of Stocks

Before you trade, you need to know the types of stocks and be able to identify them when you see them. Each kind of stock has its own uniqueness, advantages and disadvantages. You need to match each kind of stock with the investment strategy that fits it and your risk capabilities. I.e. do you want to be more speculative or play it safe at the cost of less returns?

1. **Blue Chip Stock**

This is a stock that is considered safer compared to other stocks. Blue chip companies are typically well established in their field and enjoy favorable financial conditions. They also pay dividends on a more standard schedule. They are the large cap companies. While they are generally considered safe, if the market falls they tend to follow. These stocks are what you would add to a portfolio to mitigate risks.

2. **Preferred Stock**

This is a type of stock that has a mix of stock and bond characteristics. It offers fixed dividends, as well as price appreciation. It differs from traditional stocks as traditional stocks don't offer fixed dividends, only occasional dividends. Preferred stocks however, don't appreciate as well as traditional stocks, but preferred stockholders will be paid before common stock holders in the event the company is liquidated.

3. **Dividend Stock**

Just as the name suggests, these are stocks of companies that generally pay out dividends. Not all stocks pay out dividends. In fact, many don't. These stocks generally pay out increasing dividends each year. They differ from preferred stocks since their dividends aren't fixed or guaranteed.

4. **Penny Stock**

This is a high risk, low priced stock that is typically shunned by the general investing crowd, except for those who really know what they're doing. Technically, stocks that trade under a price of $5 per share are considered penny stocks. These are stocks of companies that would be considered risky but have great yields IF it works out. They might be unestablished or poorly performing companies. One of the main drawbacks of these stocks, aside from the risk, is that they are not very liquid. This means that if you want to sell your shares, you might have a hard time finding buyers right away. Or you will have to sell them at a huge loss.

5. **Growth Stock**

These are stocks of companies with earnings that are expected to increase, compared to the general stock market. These stocks typically don't pay dividends. Instead of paying dividends, a company will spend their extra profits on reinvesting the money back into the company, so they can continue to grow. Earnings refer to revenue minus expenses for a company.

6. **Value stock.**

These are stocks that trade lower than their perceived value. These stocks generally pay dividends, and are found by the use of fundamental analysis techniques, which we will get into soon.

Before you invest I advise you do the following:

1. **Understand your current financial standings**
   This helps you to know how much you own and owe. It also helps you to know how much money you have free for investment. Determining your financial standing involves creating a personal financial statement. The financial statement has been discussed earlier. Don't over commit funds you can't afford to be tied up in stock investments. Stocks are medium to long term investment instruments after all.

2. **Gather your money together**
   Make sure you have more than enough money in reserve. Make sure there is an emergency fund you can fall on. I will

advise you to have at least, four times your monthly income saved up as a cash deposit. List your assets in order of liquidity so you can determine the assets you can easily convert into cash if you run out of capital.

3. **Determine your risk level**
You have to know how much you are willing to lose if things don't go the way you want. I advise that you create red flags at thresholds. If the market falls to a particular point that you are not willing to go beyond? Sell your stocks, even if you have made a loss. Taking a risk beyond your capacity can be dangerous. Resist the temptation to hold on to failing stocks. Although it may rebound in the future? Your capital is tied up to those assets. Lost of opportunity costs or that capital you could reinvest elsewhere to make more profits. Ultimately you will have to determine if riding it out till things get better OR change horses and invest elsewhere is more beneficial.

4. **Study the market**
Like I have said earlier, you need to be able to study the market very carefully, no shortcuts and form a trend over a period of time. Trends are usually influenced by market indicators. Study these indicators to know the cause of the trend you are seeing in the market. For instance, if the S & P 500 keeps increasing steadily, it means market capitalization is getting bigger and the market is in a bullish period. But you need to know the particular company to invest in. Study the industries and pick an industry that is performing well. Check out the biggest losers and gainers in the industry. Pick out a few companies and concentrate on them. Study these companies and their owners and decide whether they are big or small companies (based on cap), stable or unstable (based on internal and external events). There are many more and I advise you to read and learn as much as humanly possible, because the world of stock market investing is filled with MBAs, Economics and Finance professionals and other experts. Don't be afraid to seek their input. Even the seasoned

veterans have a team of experts at their beck and call, to help them pick stocks.

5. **Determine your investment strategy**
   Your investment strategy will determine your approach to investing. Once you known your risk factors and you understand the market, you can follow the investment strategy that suits your goals. Do you want to go through companies' statement of accounts and select stocks that trade for less than their actual value (fundamental) or you would rather go through the stocks chart and find short term trading opportunities(technical trading). Or have you come across a special and significant piece of information you know will greatly impact share prices? There are many factors in decision making with stocks.

Stocks Investment Strategies

Fundamental/Value Investing

Value investing is a strategy of selecting stocks that trade for less than their actual value. Value investors actively seek stocks of companies they believe the market has undervalued. This entails reading financial statements and using fundamental analysis. By carrying out fundamental analysis, experts endeavor to determine a security's value by focusing on primary factors that affect a company's *actual* business and its future growth prospects. They focus on analyzing a company's financial statements and performance.

Technical Trading

This occurs when investors see if they can find short term trading opportunities, typically with the use of stock charts. To give you an idea of how a technical analyst makes decisions, let's take a look at a very basic technical analysis strategy. Many analysts believe that the best time to invest in a stock is when the stock's price is above its

200 Day Moving Average. The 200 Day Moving Average is the average of prices over the last 200 days of trading. Most charting software will have an add-on for the 200 Day Moving Average. So if you were looking at a line chart of prices over time, say a year, you would see how the price is doing compared to its 200 Day Moving Average. The price line is created by the price each day. The 200 Day Moving Average line is made up of the 200 Day average price each day, assuming it is being calculated each day. So a technical analyst would look at the chart, and if the stock price is greater than its current 200 Day Moving Average, it would be a good time to buy. That is just one indicator. There are hundreds of indicators out there that technical analysts use, but the 200 Day Moving Average is a good example.

Short Selling

The strategy of short selling occurs when you sell a security that you do not own. Short sellers assume that they will be able to buy the stock at a lower amount than the price at which they sold short. When you short sell a stock, your broker will lend it to you. You must close the short by buying back the same number of shares and returning them to your broker. So if the price drops, you can buy back the stock at the lower price and make a profit on the difference. If the price of the stock rises, you have to buy it back at the higher price, in which case you lose money. You will need a **Margin Account** to sell stocks short. A margin account lets the broker lend you a portion of the funds at the time of purchase and the security acts as collateral. There is no limit to how much you can lose if the stock rises rapidly.

What to look out for

To exploit market inefficiency for a stock, you must understand the value of that stock and the story behind the business.

Certain things usually influence our stock investment decisions

1. **Stock valuation**: The first thing that you need to pay attention to is the value of a stock. The price of this stock is going to be determined by the activity in the market around it. When you want to determine whether it is a good time to purchase, is to look at its actual price compared to the fair value price. For example, if the stock is worth $35 and it is being traded at $30, it may be worth your time to purchase. There are different ways to determine this though. You can look at the intrinsic value of the company or go through the balance sheets and crunch all the numbers. You may need to work with a stock market professional to help you come up with the right formula for purchasing stocks.

2. **Triggering event**: if you have a good understanding of the triggering event, you will be able to notice it coming and move your assets somewhere else before it plummets and you lose all of your money. Learn about these triggering events early on to save yourself from heartaches.

3. **Human decision process**: humans do not always react in the same way as the numbers show. You may go into a decision logically, but when a stock starts to slide, or something big happens with a company, the emotions can start to take over. You need to understand how human emotions can come into play when picking out a stock and how this can either make you money or lose money in the process.

Financial Advisors

You may want to take a financial advisor while investing in stocks. The financial advisor is the professional that spends his time studying the market on your behalf, giving you sound advice on what to invest in, when to buy and when to sell. One of the advantages of having a financial advisor is that he is an expert in stocks, unlike you who has another profession but is just learning the ropes on stock trading. Your financial advisor is going to be the one who is on your side during the whole investing process. They are in charge of explaining the different investments, watching your stocks and discussing if it may be time to make some changes when a company starts to do poorly, and the person you go to if you have any questions. This can take a lot of the pressure off your shoulders and will help you to make some of the smartest decisions when it comes to your stock market options.

Things to consider when choosing a financial advisor:

- Knowledge and experience
- How he will be compensated
- His attitude
- Compatibility with your investment goals

Getting Started

Getting into stocks is not a difficult process. You simply need to choose the broker that you want to use and pick the right stocks and get started. You can easily transfer money and as long as you make some good decisions and don't jump ship all of the time (remember those broker fees for trades as well), you will see success and make some great money! You can follow the following steps as a beginner.

Open a Brokerage Account

The first thing that you will need to do in order to purchase stocks is to open up your account. You will need to find a discount broker and then sign up online to have stocks. Take a look at the different fees that the broker is going to charge. Some will have a lot higher fees compared to others and you could be losing money if you don't do your research. On the other hand, these expensive brokers may have value added services you won't find on lower tier brokerage firms.

Fund Your Account

Now that the account is set up, you will need to put some money into the account. This is pretty easy to do as you just choose the right amount you want to use and either send in a check or transfer right from your bank account. The check will take a bit longer but most brokers will be fine in using it.

Select Your Stocks

Once you have your money in the account, it is time to figure out which stocks you would like to procure. If you are doing this with a financial advisor, they will be able to look at your goals and help you find the right stocks to make money with. They can pick out a few options, watch the trends for you, and help you make some important decisions to get the best profit. If you are doing it on your own, you will need to be proactive and watch the different stocks to make sure you are picking the right ones to make a profit.

Diversify

If you are a beginner, you should diversify your portfolio a bit. It is never a good idea to put all of your money in just one stock. Buy different stocks from different industries. Diversifying your portfolio limits your risk. Sure, you could make a lot of money if the stock does well, but if it does poorly, you could end up losing it all in one swoop.

So pick at least two or three stocks to divide your money in. This way, if one stock does poorly, you still have the others to hold you up and making you money.

Be Patient and Optimistic

The stock market is always fluctuating. You usually don't have a continuous increase or decrease without some ups and downs.

This is why even as a beginner, you need to stick with the investment. This can be hard right in the beginning. You are excited to make a lot of money and may feel like you aren't earning fast enough. Some people aren't willing to stick for ten years or more with one stock in the hopes of earning some good money. But if you want to really make good money with this investment, you need to get into the stock market now and stay with it for the long term. This is when the best returns come into play.

WHILE YOU ARE INVESTING

Now that you know what it takes to invest in stocks, we need to go into the trading process.

I have classified stocks trading into 5 types based on duration:

Day Trading

Day trading is a type of investing where you will buy and then sell your stocks all on the same day. The trading will need to close before the market has closed down for the day. If you are a trader who goes in on this day trading, you are called an active trader. This is a good option if you would like the ability to make money quickly and you are able to take fast action while making decisions right away.

This is a tough kind of trading and it is not recommended for those who are just getting into the stock market. Most stocks are going to see growth over time, but if you are following the stock for just a day, you may see a dramatic decrease during this time. As a day trader, you need to have a good understanding of how the market works and be able to recognize trends enough to stay on top of it all.

There are a few different methods that you can use when going with day trading. These methods include:

- **Arbitrage:** This can be helpful in capturing slight changes in the price. When there are differences in prices of a stock which is located on two different places, the trader would pick the one that is lower priced and then sell it on the higher priced market. For this one, you will look at two or more places for the stock. If they are all the same price, it doesn't make sense to purchase it. But if you can find it for a lower price, you would make the purchase and sell it on the other site right away for a higher price to make a profit.

- **Market making:** The stock exchanges are going to appoint the market makers and will be the ones who provide `ask and bid' rates to the brokers when buying and selling stocks on the big exchange sites.

- **Momentum day trading:** This is a type of stock trading where a certain trade is made while the stock is trending in movement and then the trade will close down at the end of the market day.

- **Pattern trading:** As the price of the stock goes up and down, you will start to notice a pattern over time and can even see them on the charts. You will be able to use pattern trading to determine if your day stock is going up or down so you can act accordingly.

- **Scalping**: This method involves getting small profits quickly from hundreds of trades during the day. You will use the '**ask and bid**' differences given to you and make a ton of trades all day long. You will not make a ton of money off each stock, but overall, with so many trades, you are going to see a profit.

- **Price action trading**: With this method, you will only consider the price actions. You will need to decide on a time period from 1 to 60 minutes, and then you will trade it during that day. You will simply look at the open, high, low, and then close during that time period to make money.

- **Rebate trading**: This is a day trading method where you will be paid by your service provided for buying and selling stocks.

- **News playing:** This is a method where you will follow the news releases that show up during the day. You will decide to buy and sell based on these news releases and it is going to be closed within one day as well.

Short Term Trading

This is similar to day trading, but you are going to have more than a day to get it done. It is usually between two days and a few weeks for trading. For this type, you will purchase a stock and then hold onto it for a day up to two weeks. After this time, you will sell it again, hopefully for a nice profit. This kind of trade is entered when you create a sell position, which will then be covered later on. Pattern trading and swig trading are good examples of how this works.

Medium Trading

This is where we get into the longer term trading options for the stock market. This is usually going to last anywhere from a few weeks to a few months. The trend here is followed with tailoring any stop loss. Swing trading and Elliot wave trading are good to use when you want to stick with medium trading. This one is a good option if you would like to follow the trends a bit more but don't want to work with the stocks for too long.

Long Term Trading

This kind of trading can last anywhere from a few months to many years. If you have a retirement account, you are probably playing with long term trading because the stocks are going to basically stay put for a long time to come. You will see a lot less risk with this option because you have time to go through the different progressions of the stock and will generally earn a good profit.

Warning

All stocks go through periods of ups and downs. That is just how business works. If you are sticking with some of the shorter term trading options listed above, you may be hit with some of the downturns of a particular stock without much time to come back when the stock prices go back up. With long term investing, you may lose some money temporarily, but you can also see big gains in your money. When you stick with a stock for the long term, you are generally going to come out way ahead than you started.

Talk to your financial advisor about going with a longer term option if this seems like it would fit your overall goals.

Making the Right Investment

To make a reliable profit from investing, you must understand two things well: what a stock is worth and what other people are willing to pay for it. Only then can you decide whether a specific opportunity is worth pursuing. Is now a good time to invest? If you've found a good opportunity, the answer is always yes!

For you to make money any profitable investment has to increase in value somehow. If you buy a stock for $1 and sell it for $2, you've made money.

When to Buy:

1. **When a Company's Stock is Undervalued**
   When you know the stock price of a company is lower than its book value, there is huge potential for growth in the future. This is like the opposite of a bubble, whereby a company's stock is trading higher than its real value. If you notice that a company's stock is undervalued, buy and watch patiently as market forces drive the price up in the future. You can know this from careful study of the company and analysis of its financial statement. If you are doing short term investment, you may not be able to do this.

2. **When a Company is Growing**
   If you have seen remarkable recent growth in a company's size, profit and stability -- you need to buy fast. Remember, many other investors are studying the company just as you are doing. If they start buying before you, the price will start increasing. That is why you need to start investing early, but not too early. To minimize risk, you can have a predetermined threshold.

3. **When Stock Price Rises to Your "Buy Price"**
   Since you cannot always predict accurately if a stock's price will continue to rise indefinitely or fall soon, you need to set up a range of value at which you buy a stock. For instance, if the stock price shows a rise of 5% within a week, and you can relate the increase to an increase in the company's growth, you can buy it in the second week after it rises from $21 to 22$

4. **When a Company is Strong**
   Very big and strong companies are known as blue chips. The reason why the prices of blue chip stocks keep rising is because people keep buying them and people keep buying them because they trust that they are stable. These companies have weathered the storms in the past and have come out stronger. Therefore, investors believe they will show resilience. If you are investing in the long term and interested in security, buy into a strong company and watch your investment grow steadily into the future.

When to Sell:

When You Realize You Have Bought in Error

If you suddenly discover that you made a mistake while purchasing a stock, you need to sell it quickly. If you realize that while buying the stock you made an error in judgment or you have bought it for the wrong reasons, you need to sell it fast. It is a bad stock. The key to successful investing is to rely on data, strategy and analysis -- and not on your emotional swings. If the analysis you carried out before buying is flawed? You will only make more mistakes if you hold on to it because you do not have control over it. The stock price may go up after you sell, but you won't be able to predict correctly, what will happen to it in the future. It is true that everyone makes mistakes but learning from a mistake that costs you a 10% loss on your investment could be one of the best investment decisions you could make.

When There is a Significant Rise

It is true that nobody can totally predict the market. Therefore, you may never know when a stock has reached its highest or lowest value. When a stock you bought for less is appreciating fast and it gets to the point you are comfortable with selling it. A cheap stock can become an expensive stock in a very short period of time for a host of reasons, some of which are likely due to speculation by others. Take your gains and move on.

To make it easier, always plan from the outset, the limit of appreciation; that is the highest value the stock will get to before you sell. For instance, you can say that for every 10% increase in the value of a certain stock, you will sell 50% of your stocks.

When What Initially Drew You to the Company has Changed Dramatically.

This usually applies to long term investments. We usually put our money in certain companies because they have certain qualities that guarantee security, growth and profit. These qualities may include stability, strong financial records and large market cap. When these things begin to change, it is time to review your investments.

Sometimes the change is not significant enough to make you sell, but sometimes it is. For instance if you bought into ExxonMobil due to its long-term stability, strength, size and market cap and the company is suddenly acquired? You will be the one to review your investment. If the new owner starts laying off workers and there is a lot of negative publicity, or the company starts losing money? It is time to sell. Note that other investors in the company are studying the same things as you, and if they begin to sell before you -- you will start noticing a drop in the stock prices. Sell immediately, before you start incurring a loss. Follow your guts, but also be cautious.

If you think the company can still bounce back, you may not want sell all your shares. You can retain 30-40% for future trading. Another reason to sell is bankruptcy. If this happens, sell all your stocks immediately, without looking back.

When There is a Noticeable Dip in Stock Price

There is no reason to keep a losing stock. When you notice that your stock is losing value rapidly, sell it before it falls below the price you bought it. If you bought it at a higher price and you have already made a loss -- sell it immediately before your loss hits 10% so that your loss doesn't multiply. However, if other factors point to the ability of the company stocks to rebound or the market is in a bullish trend, you may retain a few stocks; let's say in the 30% range. Ultimately, the decision must be based on your risk tolerance. You should decide before you purchase the stocks how much you would like to see the stock grow and how much you are willing to lose on the investment.

Bad Investment Behaviors

Now you have started investing. You know when to buy and when to sell. There are however, certain habits you need to avoid to be a successful stocks investor.

Getting addicted to a particular stock
Do not get emotionally attached to a particular stock. While being an emotional venture, stocks investment should not be controlled by emotions. Don't attach sentimental value to any stock. The best investments may do well for a long while, and accrue considerable wealth, but every stock has its end, and the best investors also know when it is time to cash out.

Chasing a losing stock

As stated earlier in the book, you need to have a threshold for loss; the amount of money you can afford to lose. Also don't buy a losing stock. When you've seen a stock deteriorate steadily and you can't point out a recent event that can turn around the trend-- stay away!

Following the wrong info
As stated earlier, don't follow the headlines, follow the trend lines. Don't trade on anonymous tips. Take time to study the market and not just listen to locker room talk. Don't just act on what you receive from the media, it can be misleading sometimes. Instead, consider all factors that can affect your stocks of interest.

Greed
Greed makes you want to make maximum profit at all cost. Stocks investment is not a gamble; it is a cautious endeavour -- though fraught with risks. Greed is dangerous because it will not allow you to dump a stock when you should because you are waiting endlessly for the price to shoot high into the heavens. Greed can likewise make you buy too early because you want to outsmart other investors.

Conclusion

It is my belief that after reading this book, you have gained insights into what to do before investing and how to invest. The world of stocks investment is both simple and complicated. It is simple for those who enter it with the right knowledge while it is complicate for those who don't have the requisite knowledge. This isn't just a game for the ultra-wealthy. In addition to saving and making sure you have enough money for your everyday expenses, planning for long-term objectives such as retirement, education or a large purchase is essential. The lessons I have given you can help you get started, but your journey isn't over. This book is just an introduction or a primer. You will need to deep dive and study in depth, the concepts laid out in the book.

I would also like to emphasize the value of simulations. This is virtual trading with play money, using real world market data. Only when you have acquired all the necessary tools and experiences, should you go into the riskier areas of stock investing. If you really must? You can go ahead and invest in the safest investment options. But don't undermine the value of actually making money through correct decision making. And you will not get to this level, except with a lot of practice. Practice you can get with simulations or having a small capital entirely for the purpose of getting your feet wet and gaining experience.

Thank you for reading.

Thanks again for your support!

- Neil

The authors, publishers, and distributors of this guide have made every effort to ensure the validity, accuracy, and timely nature of the information presented here However, no guarantee is made, neither direct nor implied, that the information in this guide or the techniques described herein are suitable for or applicable to any given individual person or group of persons, nor that any specific result will be achieved The authors, publishers, and distributors of this guide will be held harmless and without fault in all situations and causes arising from the use of this information by any person, with or without professional medical supervision The information contained in this book is for informational and entertainment purposes only It not intended as a professional advice or a recommendation to act

No part of this book may be reproduced or transmitted in any form whatsoever, electronic, or mechanical, including photocopying, recording, or by any informational storage or retrieval system without express permission from the author

© Copyright 2016, JNR Publishing

All rights reserved

Other books by JNR Publishing Group

Real Ways to Make Money Online:
How to make money at home on the internet for beginners

Investing in Stock Market for Beginners: Understanding the basics in how to make money with stocks.

The Best Real Estate Book For Beginners: Training In The Game Of Real Estate Investments

Develop Powerful Business Thinking and Reasoning Processes
Hit the Ground Running in Business
Learn Must know Business Fundamentals for the New Entrepreneur
Conflicting Views
Tactfully handle any conflicts in any organization

The Fine Art of Decision Making
Make things happen by making the right calls!

SAMPLE CHAPTERS:

The Best Real Estate Book For Beginners: Training In The Game Of Real Estate Investments

A Passive Investor:

Not every real estate investor wants to be hands on. If you prefer, you can be a passive investor and take the back seat. There are people who are not willing to be aggravated by the daily hassles of real estate operations. These include:

Real estate investment trusts (REITs):

There are two categories of REITs (real estate investment trusts). There are property REITs (also known as equity REITs) which are profit making companies that manage the different properties they own. These properties range from hotel buildings to shopping malls, among other rentals. The other category is mortgage REITs which are more inclined towards financing investors by lending them money or offering mortgage back securities. REITs are also either public which means they are traded on the stock exchange and provide full disclosure of their activities and fees. Or they can be private, and in this case they are not compelled to full disclosure of their activities. Since your investment in under the REIT, you have very little contact with the daily real estate hassles.

Tenants in Common (TIC):

This is whereby several people join together under the sponsorship of Tenants in common investment group (TIC). You get a title deed to your share of the larger investment. This option, gives you the opportunity to invest in prime property without having to absorb all the costs on your own. However, you are responsible for the debts, just as you are entitled to enjoy the profits. Unfortunately, in case of a loss -- you can't count on the TIC to bail you out as per the terms and conditions. To have a smooth venture, you must work out issues such as:

How do the commissions get shared out and who are the beneficiaries? How much is the property management fee and how easy is it to liquidate your share of the property?

Triple Net Properties:

In this form of real estate, a tenant is responsible in part or in whole for the expenses of maintaining the property. These are a favorite for investors who want to dodge the headaches of real estate. Most Fast food and restaurant franchises opt for this real estate option because the property is built to the specifications of their business. However, you must decide what responsibilities lie with the landlord and with the tenant. You must also keep an eye on the maintenance of the property and also make sure you are named in the tenant's insurance coverage just to safe guard your investment.

Notes and trust deeds:

This is when instead of buying property and developing it? You become the lender to people who want to buy and develop properties. You purchase notes and trust deeds that have the security interest given to real estate investors to protect them from foreclosure because of nonpayment. These security interests are called pledged real estate. Although it puts you in the position of making quite a bit of coin, you run the risk of being left with the legal fees and the cost of foreclosure in addition to the unpaid loan should the borrower default.

Tax Lien Certificate Sales:

This is a legal claim against a property owner for not satisfactorily meeting the payment obligations on his property. When you buy a tax lien certificate, you are actually settling the government taxes on behalf of the property owner and buying the rights to collect that amount from him. He can continue to stay on the property and maintain it as he makes his payments to you. Make sure you only buy tax lien certificates for properties you are happy to own.

Limited Partnerships:

This is when you have no role in the management of the properties and unlike the general partner who accepts unlimited liability? You are only responsible for the losses on your investment. In this situation, there is a general partner who is actively in charge of everything --even deciding on the sale of a given property. As a passive partner you have no authority on these kinds of decisions, so you must be careful to partner with someone who is honest, responsible and trustworthy.

Fast Money; Truth or Scam

The unfortunate reality of real estate is the need for a lump sum to start off and the need for real profits and returns after investing --especially because of the huge amount of money you had to put up to begin with. Because of this, scammers trying to give you fast money property deals are rife in this industry. Unfortunately, fast money and real estate rarely go together. But to steer clear of these kinds of deals, you have to understand why you are cautioned against them. For example, it is very hard to find a seller who will pay you to take a property unless they are trying to get rid of a property with major problems. Once in a while, you may find honest sellers who have good properties and need to dispose of them quickly. This could be because they are relocating, have an emergency or are unable to afford its upkeep anymore. But even when you come across this criterion of people, you have to keenly assess whether they are being truthful or not. In such cases, you are definitely on to a good buy and you may not need to even deposit some money. if the seller does hire you? You will dispose off his property because of his urgency.

If after reading the above you still want to invest in properties that don't require you to put money down at the beginning? Then your best option will be retirees with whom you can come to an arrangement of paying in installments to ensure a steady income spread over time. Or people who have inherited properties but want to dispose of it but don't want a lump sum. They instead prefer installments for a steady income. To make good returns off no money down properties, you need to apply the buy and flip strategy. The buy, flip and refinance strategy is a winner because you can renovate a property and sell it off at a much higher value after buying it at a much lower one.

Your Real Estate Team

As you can see, there is a lot of work that goes into a real estate venture. To succeed and excel at it-- you must have a strong team behind you. Because real estate is a multi prong venture that requires strong negotiation skills, financial acumen and an in depth understanding of the economy and the growth prospects. You have to find people with such skills to help you achieve your goals. Before even looking at a property, let alone buying it, ensure you have the right team of people. This team will help you close deals faster because they will conduct the due diligence and they have the expertise to recognize a sound investment when they see it. Your team should comprise of:

A Tax Advisor: This is a crucial team member who can pinpoint tax issues that will benefit you or pit falls in your potential investment. A tax advisor with real estate experience is more equipped to notice things in the fine print.

A Financial Advisor: This is someone with experience in financial planning for real estate investors. Keep away from commission hunting financial advisors because they are not very objective.

A Mortgage Broker or a Lender: A mortgage broker is someone who will look for the best lending institutions to match your needs and they will go to them as your representative to find financing for your ventures. A lender on the other hand is an institution that give loans to investors to buy real estate. Make sure you have a good rapport with your lender by sticking to your agreement at all times.

Real Estate Brokers and Agents: There are many rogue ones but it is an essential role in any real estate venture. This is someone who is qualified to make real estate transactions and knows the listings of properties in a given area. Look for a full time broker who understands the area and type of investments you want. Make sure they get along with you and other stake holders and also are good negotiators to ensure smooth transactions.

An Appraiser: An appraiser brings the knowledge of things surrounding a property that will translate to increasing its value in the future. He can see the hidden potential of the property by studying the geography of the area, its current value against its potential value and what the market is like in the area.

An Attorney: When you are dabbling in small rental properties, an attorney may not be a necessity but as you get into more complex deals, the services of a real estate attorney become imperative. Having an attorney check the transaction documents before you commit to anything can end up saving you from legal tussles in the future. There is also legal jargon and things in fine print that you may not understand and need an attorney to decipher for you. Look for attorneys with experience in landlord and tenant laws and commercial leases.

BONUS: Sample pages of the book

Real Ways to Make Money Online

How to make money at home on the internet for beginners

Social Media Marketing

This is the modern SEO. It's not actually SEO, but for the newbies this is much easier way to get traffic (more traffic = more sales). Which one has more potential to make sales; an ad that get's read 10 times or 10,000 times?

By Social Media we mean Facebook Groups, Facebook Fan Pages, Twitter, Youtube, Pinterest, Instagram, LinkedIn, Reddit etc.

Social Media marketing requires more finesse and definitely the opposite of blatant selling that we do on Classified ads sites. Here's just a brief overview.

Facebook

Create a Fanpage (for example about Depression, if your selling a course on that topic)

Find VIRAL memes or helpful articles or videos.

Post it on your fanpage.

Right click on date of post to get the permalink or url to spread.

Join Depression Groups (You can join 100 groups per day just to be safe)

SHARE the permalink.

Add something like "Do you agree? Please like and share to your wall if this is you"

Done!

The idea is you're just sharing useful, valuable content. A certain portion of those people will be curious and click and like your FB Page. That page should have the actual product for sell, pinned up on top. That's were you can be very sale-y on your post. But never the actual content you share! They consider that SPAM and you'll get banned soon enough.

Instagram and Twitter

It's practically the same. You share good content with the potential to get viral or shared. Use proper hashtags. And like as many as you can in Instagram. In Twitter you can tag them, but you can't go overboard.

Pinterest, it's about sharing good pictures and changing the links to your website. So if they click the link to the repined picture? It goes to your site, instead of theirs.

Ultimately, whatever type of Social media you're doing? Always DON'T SPAM! Share, share share value! Whatever value means for your audience, or that platform, just share and get viral. A portion of those people are bound to see your main ads. Another way of saying this is just be sneaky, not pushy. Never hardsell, just softsell.

Each platform requires a separate course. Above was just a preview of how it's done. Those information you can find on ebooks, google, Youtube.For more sophisticated tactics, you can learn them for free at blackhatworld.com and similar internet marketing forum.

Another thing I'd like to add, is instead of selling your products directly? You can sell the service of posting on their behalf. Fill an entire page, schedule to post content automatically for weeks or months.

You can also sell PAGE LIKES, Shares, Followers etc. Whatever it is, at some point you will have consider automation tools.

I personally use:

Social Autobot

Octosuite.com

Slacksocial.com

Massplanner.com

facedominator.com

tweetattackspro.com

ninjapinner.com

Ninjagram (ninjapinner.com)

Pinterest Blaster

(Although Social Autobot and Octosuite works? Everyone hates the creator. If you develop problems, they simply won't help you! No customer service or after sales support to depend on.)

Slack social is good, but it won't post everywhere.

Many more tools are available

Freelancing

Freelance writing, forex trading and online marketing are among the common methods to make money. Unlike the traditional forms of employment, online opportunities are easily accessible provided you have internet access. You can freelance almost anything!

Content Writing

As a content provider, you need to produce relevant information for websites. The requester submits the provider or writer with a brief on the topic to be addressed, format and keywords to be used in the content. You then create material that will engage and inform the reader. Fluency and accuracy are important features in content writing and among the basic qualities you need to succeed in the field. There are sub groups and specialties to this as well. Some articles are writing for information, others purely for SEO and others meant to persuade. For content meant to persuade, you need to train yourself in Copywriting and some psychology and NLP knowhow are strong advantages. SEO requires basic SEO knowledge. Information articles, just require one to be good at research.

Ghost Writing

Ghost writing entails producing content on behalf of another person. The requester provides the topic to be researched and written along with detailed instructions to follow. Upon successful completion of the given task, the requester makes the agreed payments for the work done. As a ghost writer, you have no rights to submitted content and the requester reaps all the benefits of the work done. For you to be a ghost writer, you need good grammar and expertise or at least strong research skills to write nonfictions. Fiction writers are a special breed. Not everyone can write good fiction and entails competence in a lot of fiction writing techniques. In some cases the client creates the story, but you flesh out the details. High caliber writers can also get jobs as proofreaders and editors due to their high competence in the craft. Normal content writers are not as good and won't make good editors and proofreaders. They just write without knowing style and grammar rules.

Graphic Design

Graphic design is the art of creating visual compositions. Expertise to use visual arts, typography and page layouts are required to succeed as a graphic designer. Opportunities in graphic design are available during production of newspapers, books and magazines. The requester sends you instructions on the type of design required including size, colors, fonts and applications to use in producing the content. Specs are also provided where exactly the materials will be used for. Print persuasion to sell more books or sell more cars on a website will be vastly different.

Please note there's a difference between graphic design and the digital arts. Graphic design gigs are different from jobs requiring expertise in Photoshop or picture manipulation.

If you possess either or both skill, you can find a lot of opportunities in Fiverr and elsewhere. A ton of people want to look amazing in their profile pictures and Facebook (Photoshop retouching), while others want good book covers or what have you.

Virtual Assistant

Virtual assistance is a service provided for individuals, small firms and businesses. It is a service where a client contracts your services to handle and help with their processes. Communication equipment and internet connections are required for the job. In some instances, you actually need to operate softwares owned by the client. You will be given their private server's username and password, and run the software. In other situations, you will be doing work on your own but the client will be constantly monitoring your work. It may also be results based, where they won't care how long it took you to do the job, just as long as you complete the assignment before the deadline. Softwares exist where a client can take dynamic snapshots of your computer screen as you do your assigned tasks. Although most clients would not require this.